EXPLAINED

THE BERMUDA TRIANGLE

BY ADAM STONE

BELLWETHER MEDIA · MINNEAPOLIS, MN

Are you ready to take it to the extreme?
Torque books thrust you into the action-packed world
of sports, vehicles, mystery, and adventure. These books
may include dirt, smoke, fire, and dangerous stunts.
WARNING : read at your own risk.

Library of Congress Cataloging-in-Publication Data

Stone, Adam.
 The Bermuda Triangle / by Adam Stone.
    p. cm. -- (Torque: The unexplained)
 Summary: "Engaging images accompany information about the Bermuda Triangle. The
combination of high-interest subject matter and light text is intended for students in grades 3
through 7"--Provided by publisher.
 Includes bibliographical references and index.
 ISBN 978-1-60014-497-4 (hardcover : alk. paper)
 1. Bermuda Triangle--Juvenile literature. 2. Shipwrecks--Bermuda Triangle--Juvenile
literature. I. Title.
 G558.S76 2010
 001.94--dc22   2010008481

This edition first published in 2011 by Bellwether Media, Inc.

Printed in the United States of America, North Mankato, MN.

080110   1162

CONTENTS

CHAPTER 1
DISAPPEARED WITHOUT A TRACE

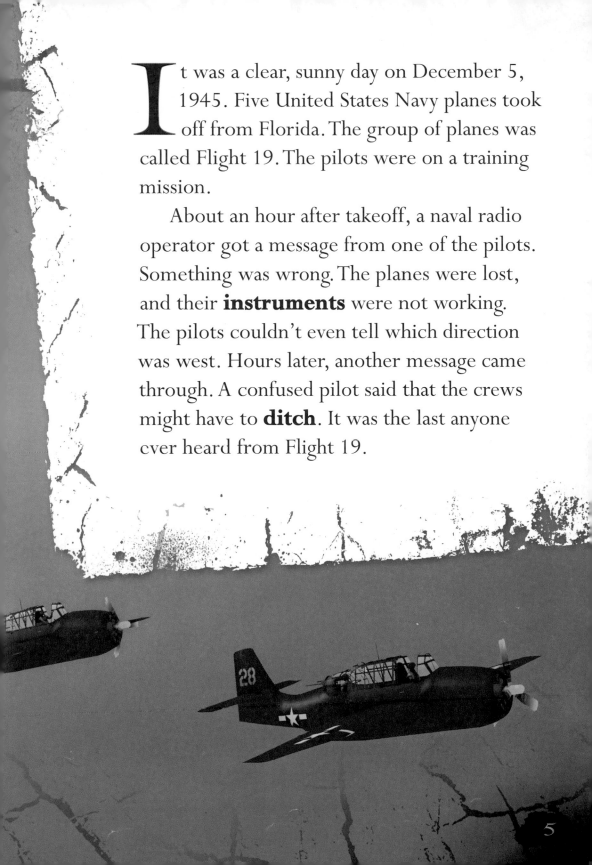

It was a clear, sunny day on December 5, 1945. Five United States Navy planes took off from Florida. The group of planes was called Flight 19. The pilots were on a training mission.

About an hour after takeoff, a naval radio operator got a message from one of the pilots. Something was wrong. The planes were lost, and their **instruments** were not working. The pilots couldn't even tell which direction was west. Hours later, another message came through. A confused pilot said that the crews might have to **ditch**. It was the last anyone ever heard from Flight 19.

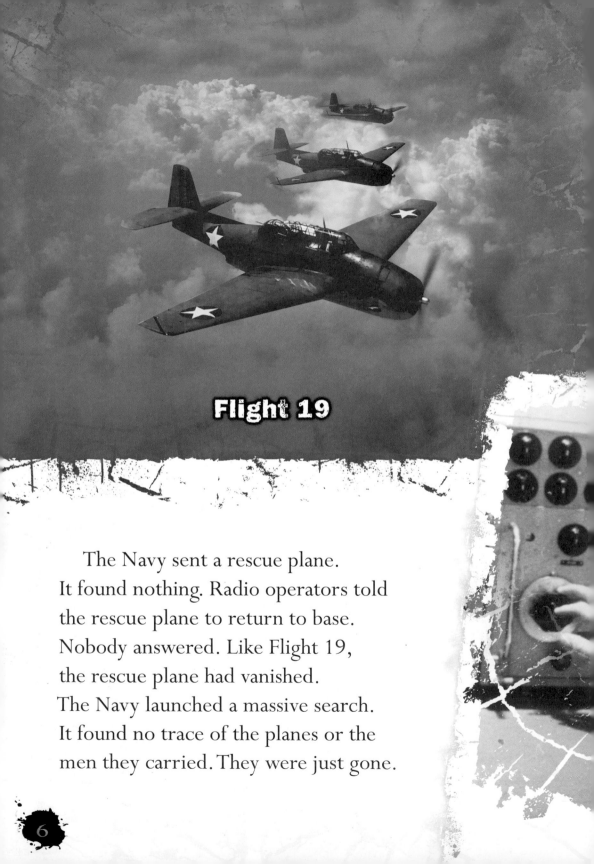

Flight 19

The Navy sent a rescue plane.
It found nothing. Radio operators told
the rescue plane to return to base.
Nobody answered. Like Flight 19,
the rescue plane had vanished.
The Navy launched a massive search.
It found no trace of the planes or the
men they carried. They were just gone.

EXPLAIN THIS

Fourteen crew members, including five experienced pilots, were aboard Flight 19. How could all five planes have gotten lost?

CHAPTER 2
THE BERMUDA TRIANGLE

Flight 19 was lost in an area known as the Bermuda Triangle. The story of Flight 19 is just one of many that come from this small patch of ocean. Dozens of ships and planes have mysteriously disappeared there.

DISAPPEARANCES IN THE BERMUDA TRIANGLE

= lost plane

= lost ship

Florida

Bermuda

Puerto Rico

The Bermuda Triangle stretches from the southern tip of Florida to the island of Puerto Rico. From there it goes north to the island of Bermuda, then back to Florida. Some people call it the Devil's Triangle. Sailors noticed something strange about this place more than 500 years ago. They called the area the Sea of Lost Ships.

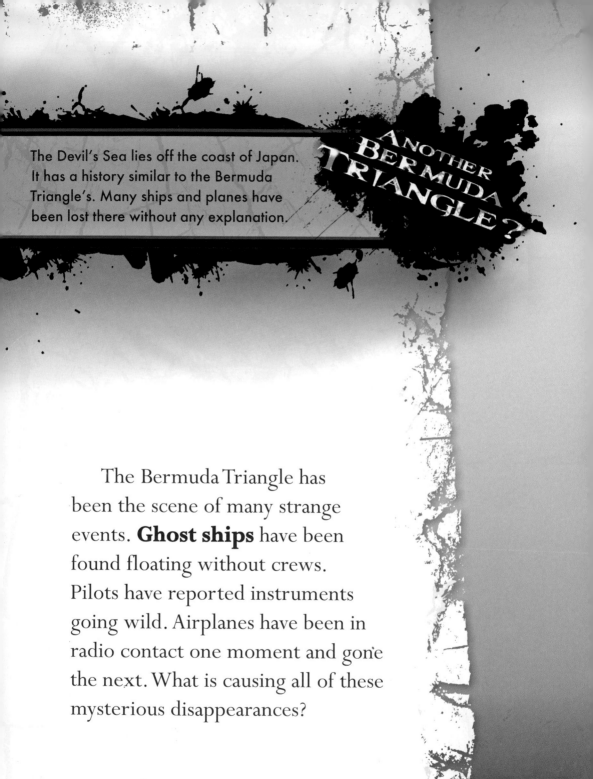

The Devil's Sea lies off the coast of Japan. It has a history similar to the Bermuda Triangle's. Many ships and planes have been lost there without any explanation.

The Bermuda Triangle has been the scene of many strange events. **Ghost ships** have been found floating without crews. Pilots have reported instruments going wild. Airplanes have been in radio contact one moment and gone the next. What is causing all of these mysterious disappearances?

HISTORY OF THE MYSTERY

Year	Ship/Plane
1840	*Rosalie*
1881	*Ellen Austin*
1918	USS *Cyclops*
1945	Flight 19
1948	*Star Tiger*
1949	*Star Ariel*
1963	KC-135 Stratotankers
1967	*Witchcraft*
1968	USS *Scorpion*
1969	Cessna
1996	*Intrepid*
1999	Cessna

What Happened

The French ship is found with all of its cargo, but no crew.

The ship is found abandoned; a new crew is assigned, and the ship again is found abandoned; a third crew disappears with the ship.

The 542-foot (165-meter) U.S. Navy ship and its crew of 309 vanish.

Five U.S. Navy planes, one rescue plane, and all crew members disappear.

The British passenger plane crashes into the ocean.

The sister plane to *Star Tiger* disappears without a trace.

Two U.S. Navy jets crash without explanation.

The small boat calls the U.S. Coast Guard for help after breaking a propeller; the Coast Guard finds no trace of the boat.

The U.S. Navy submarine disappears; it is later found on the ocean floor at a depth of 10,000 feet (3,050 meters).

A small plane flying out of Bermuda disappears.

The small boat sinks; after a distress call, no signs of life rafts or the 16 people aboard are found.

A small plane drops off of radar; no signs of survivors or wreckage are found.

CHAPTER 3
SEARCHING FOR ANSWERS

rogue wave

ROGUES on THE LOOSE

Recent studies have proven that rogue waves exist. These huge, solitary waves occur on otherwise calm seas. They can be over 80 feet (24 meters) tall!

waterspout

The mystery of the Bermuda Triangle has fascinated people for hundreds of years. There are many **theories** that try to explain the disappearances. Some people think that strong currents, **rogue waves**, lightning, or **waterspouts** sunk the ships. Human error or pirates could also be responsible.

Many people say that Earth's **magnetic field** is unstable in the Bermuda Triangle. This could cause problems with instruments. Others look for more bizarre causes. Some have blamed giant squids for pulling down ships. A few people think that aliens could have captured crew members. Some even claim that the ships and planes are traveling through time!

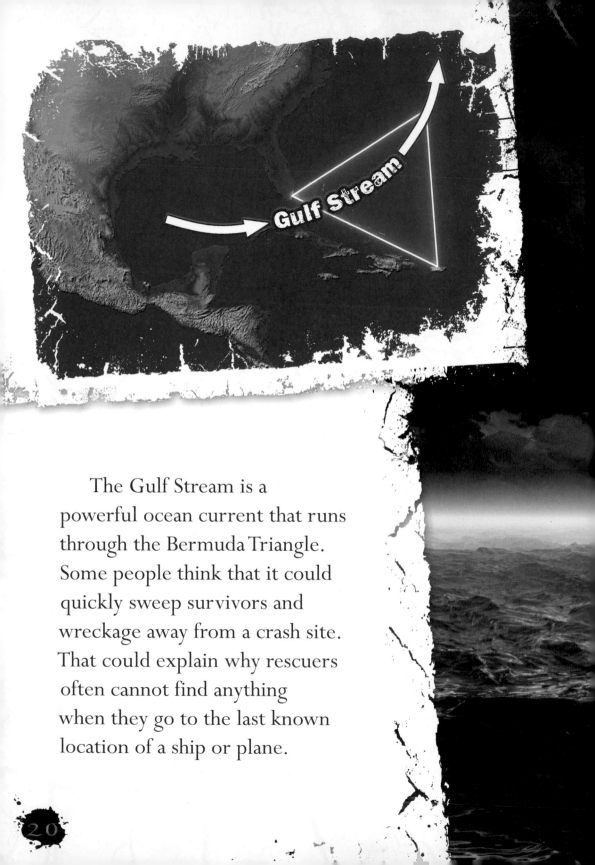

The Gulf Stream is a powerful ocean current that runs through the Bermuda Triangle. Some people think that it could quickly sweep survivors and wreckage away from a crash site. That could explain why rescuers often cannot find anything when they go to the last known location of a ship or plane.

The Bermuda Triangle holds many secrets. People will continue to try to find explanations to fit the strange disappearances. Without concrete **evidence** or eyewitness reports, it's likely the Bermuda Triangle will remain a mystery.

GLOSSARY

ditch—to attempt to land a plane on water

evidence—physical proof of something

ghost ships—ships found floating in the ocean without any crew members aboard

instruments—devices aboard a plane or ship that tell direction, speed, and more

magnetic field—the area affected by a magnet; compasses use Earth's magnetic field to determine direction.

rogue waves—huge, solitary waves that form randomly on otherwise calm seas

theories—ideas that try to explain why something exists or happens

waterspouts—tornadoes that touch down on water

TO LEARN MORE

AT THE LIBRARY

Oxlade, Chris. *The Mystery of the Bermuda Triangle*. Chicago, Ill.: Heinemann Library, 2006.

Walker, Kathryn. *Mysteries of the Bermuda Triangle*. New York, N.Y.: Crabtree Publishing, 2009.

Whiting, Jim. *The Bermuda Triangle*. Hockessin, Del.: Mitchell Lane Publishers, 2007.

ON THE WEB

Learning more about the Bermuda Triangle is as easy as 1, 2, 3.

1. Go to www.factsurfer.com.

2. Enter "Bermuda Triangle" into the search box.

3. Click the "Surf" button and you will see a list of related Web sites.

With factsurfer.com, finding more information is just a click away.

INDEX

The images in this book are reproduced through the courtesy of:
Wikipedia, front cover, pp. 4-5, 6; Getty Images, p. 7; Juan Martinez,
pp. 8-9, 17 (small), 20 (small); Jon Eppard, pp. 10-11, 18-19; Larry St.
Pierre, pp. 12-13; Carl Roessler/Photolibrary, pp. 14-15; Jens Carsten
Rosemann, pp. 16-17; Felix Mockel, pp. 20-21.